PzKpfw III in action

By Bruce Culver

Color By Don Greer

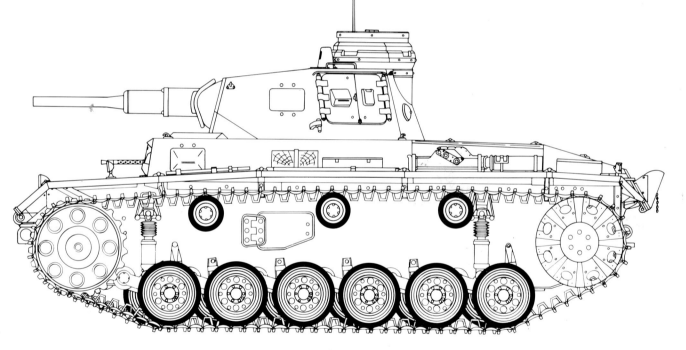

Armor Number 24

squadron/signal publications, inc.

A PzKpfw III Ausf L command tank of PzRgt 25, 7.PzDiv just prior to beginning OPERATION CITADEL, the epic tank battle to pinch off the Kursk salient in southern Russia during July of 1943.

PANZER

ASSAULT BADGE

ISBN 0-89747-199-7

If you have any photographs of the aircraft, armor, soldiers or ships of any nation, particularly wartime snapshots, why not share them with us and help make Squadron/Signal's books all the more interesting and complete in the future. Any photograph sent to us will be copied and the original returned. The donor will be fully credited for any photos used. Please send them to:

Squadron/Signal Publications, Inc.
1115 Crowley Drive.
Carrollton, TX 75011-5010.

Photo Credits

Bundesarchiv Koblenz, National Archives and Record Service (NARS) U.S. Government Official Photographs

DEDICATION

To my wife, Catharine, who never got to see this — *auf Wiedersehen*.

A PzKpfw III Ausf J of 15.PzDiv *Deutsches Afrikakorps* (DAK) is camouflaged with brush to hide it from patroling aircraft and carries the division pennant on the radio antenna. The vehicle is overall Brown, the turret number is Red outlined in White, and the name *BESTIE* is in Black.

INTRODUCTION

The *Panzerkampfwagen* III (PzKpfw III), along with the contemporary PzKpfw IV, represented a major step forward in the development of the modern main battle tank. These vehicles were the first tanks designed for use in integrated armor attacks, like those envisioned by Guderian and other farsighted leaders who understood the potential of mobile warfare.

Design contracts for the PzKpfw III and IV were issued by the German Ordnance Department to the firms of MAN, Daimler-Benz, Rheinmetall-Borsig, and Krupp in 1935. The lighter vehicle, in the 15 ton class, was originally designated the 37MM *Geschütz-Panzerwagen*, and given the number Vs Kfz 619 (Trial Vehicle 619). Later the designation was changed to *Zugführerwagen* (platoon leader's vehicle).

After evaluating designs from both Krupp and Daimler-Benz, the Ordnance Department awarded a development contract to Daimler-Benz for production of a series of prototype vehicles under the designation *Panzerkampfwagen* III with production of the first prototypes beginning in 1937.

A major design feature of the Ordnance Department specification was the provision for armor protection around the entire vehicle. Since the PzKpfw III was intended to be used in the forward element of an armored assault force, it had to be protected from enemy fire from all directions. In contrast, the heavier PzKpfw IV, intended as a fire support tank, was more heavily armored in the front than in the rear.

Daimler-Benz produced four developmental prototypes of the PzKpfw III. The 15MM armor of these vehicles was designed to protect the tank from standard anti-tank rifles then in use. Armament was specified to be a 37MM KwK cannon with a barrel length of 46.5 calibers. Secondary armament consisted of two coaxial 7.92MM MG 34 machine guns in the mantlet, and a third MG 34 in an armored ball mount in the superstructure front plate.

The PzKpfw III had a crew of five: commander, gunner, loader, driver, and radio operator/bow gunner. Early vehicles were powered by a 230 hp Maybach V-12 gasoline engine mounted in the rear of the hull coupled with a five speed gearbox and final drive unit installed in the front of the hull. The engine drive shaft ran under the vehicle floor. This basic layout of vehicle and crew set the standard for future tank development for more than a decade. Many other tanks of the mid-1930s had two or three-man crews, which often overworked the crew members. Additionally, both the PzKpfw III and IV were equipped with an intercommunications system which linked the entire crew, allowing quick and accurate orders to be passed even in the noise and confusion of combat.

Four developmental models (Ausf A-D) were used to test power train components, armament installations, and suspension designs, with each of the four service test models having a different suspension system. Service trials and limited combat service during the late 1930s revealed problems with all of the early suspension systems, and none were adopted for large scale production. These test vehicles, however, were useful in eliminating designs that were not fully suitable for combat use.

The first variant, the *Ausführung A* (model or Ausf A), had a simple suspension consisting of five large roadwheels with individual coil springs and two track return rollers on each side of the vehicle. The next three versions, the Ausf B, C, and D, used variations of a leaf spring suspension with eight small roadwheels and three return rollers on each side.

Because the early models were intended primarily for service trials and development, they were not built in large numbers. Ten Ausf As were built in 1937 followed by fifteen Ausf Bs. These were followed by fifteen Ausf C tanks in 1937-38 with thirty Ausf Ds being produced in 1938. All of these early trials variants were built by Daimler-Benz.

PANZER III AUSF A-D

The PzKpfw III Ausf A was the first of four prototype/developmental models built by Daimler-Benz after winning the design competition with Krupp. The Ausf A prototype first appeared in 1936 and was a 15.4 ton vehicle capable of twenty mph. Armor protection throughout the tank was 15MM and was intended to protect the vehicle from armor piercing anti-tank rifle ammunition (usually in the 14-20MM range). The Ausf A was intended to be a service trials vehicle and production was limited to ten vehicles (chassis numbers 60101-60110).

Many of the features that would become standard on the PzKpfw III series were introduced on the Ausf A. The basic structure consisted of four major assemblies; hull, forward superstructure, rear engine superstructure, and rotating turret. The hull and superstructure assemblies bolted together, making repair and later modification easier. The fully-rotating turret was similar in shape to that of the larger PzKpfw IV, however, the turret ring diameter of 1520MM (5 feet) was too small to mount the heavier weapons that became needed during 1943. Throughout the PzKwpf III's career, however, the interior layout of the hull and turret gave the five man crew sufficient space to perform their duties.

The combination of adequate interior space, good crew layout with specialized crew duties, good crew communications, and excellent training made the PzKpfw III and its contemporaries far superior in action to many Allied tanks that, on paper, were better designs. Indeed, the initial success enjoyed by the early PzKpfw III Ausf A-D was more a matter of training and tactics rather than technical superiority. The early PzKpfw IIIs were not true combat ready battle tanks and all were withdrawn from service by mid-1940.

All PzKpfw III variants shared the same basic mechanical layout. At the front of the hull was the transmission and final drive unit. The transmission in the Ausf A and D had six forward gears and one reverse. The transmission in the Ausf B and C had five forward gears and one reverse. The Maybach V-12 HL108TR gasoline engine was mounted in the hull rear, connected with the transmission and final drive unit through a long drive shaft which ran under the crew compartment floor.

The crew of a PzKpfw III Ausf A enjoys a meal while the tank commander confers with his superiors during German Army maneuvers held in the Winter of 1937-38. The two co-axial MG 34 machine guns were staggered to accommodate the belt feeds with the starboard armored sleeve in the mantlet being shorter than the port sleeve. (NARS)

The fully rotating turret was set over the vehicle's center of gravity in the forward upper superstructure and carried a 37MM KwK L/45 cannon. The Ausf A, B, and C had a simple drum shaped cupola, while the Ausf D had a cast armored cupola similar to that used on the PzKpfw IV Ausf B. All had the main gun and two co-axial MG 34 machine guns set into a wide mounting with an internal armored mantlet.

Each of the four early PzKpfw III models tested a different suspension system. The Ausf A had a unique chassis with five large road wheels and two small track return rollers on each side of the vehicle. The road wheels were sprung with large coil springs. This suspension proved unsuitable and in an effort to improve the suspension, three variations of leaf spring chassis designs were tested. All three designs made use of eight small road wheels and three track return rollers on each side of the vehicle.

The Ausf B used two large leaf springs, each supporting two equalized bogie trucks, with each bogie truck carrying two sets of road wheels. The Ausf C rearranged the four bogie trucks and used three leaf springs, augmented by hydraulic lever action shock absorbers. The Ausf D had a further rearrangement of the leaf springs with the end springs angled for better leverage and the shock absorbers moved toward the front and rear ends of the vehicle.

None of these suspensions proved successful, however, experience with these early production tanks provided valuable lessons for future variants. Production of all three variants was limited with fifteen Ausf Bs being built in 1937 (chassis numbers 60201-60215), fifteen Ausf Cs were produced in 1937-38 (chassis numbers 60301-60315), and two groups of fifteen Ausf D's were built in late 1938 (chassis numbers 60221-60225 and 60316-60340).

During the 1930s, Professor Ferdinand Porsche was a leading German automotive designer and a pioneer in the development of the torsion bar suspension. Daimler-Benz adapted this suspension for the chassis design of the next variant of the PzKpfw III, the Ausf E. The new chassis design was so successful that it was used on all subsequent variants of the PzKpfw III and on the self-propelled weapons that were built on the PzKpfw III chassis.

A PzKpfw III Ausf A during testing at Wunsdorf in 1938. The box-shaped superstructure, large road wheels, and coil spring suspension were the primary identification features of the Ausf A. In an effort to increase production and simplify spare parts procurement many of the mechanical fittings were common to both the PzKpfw III and Pzkpfw IV.

A Panzer III Ausf B enters an Austrian city to the cheers of the populace during the 1938 German occupation of Austria. The smoke candles mounted on the starboard muffler would become a standard feature on subsequent PzKpfw III variants.

Supsension Systems

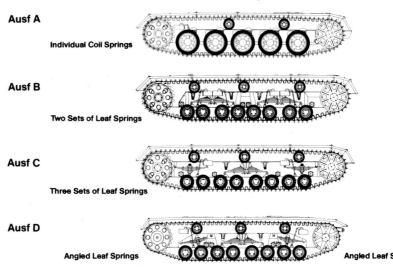

Ausf A

Individual Coil Springs

Ausf B

Two Sets of Leaf Springs

Ausf C

Three Sets of Leaf Springs

Ausf D

Angled Leaf Springs   Angled Leaf Springs

5

PzKpfw III Development

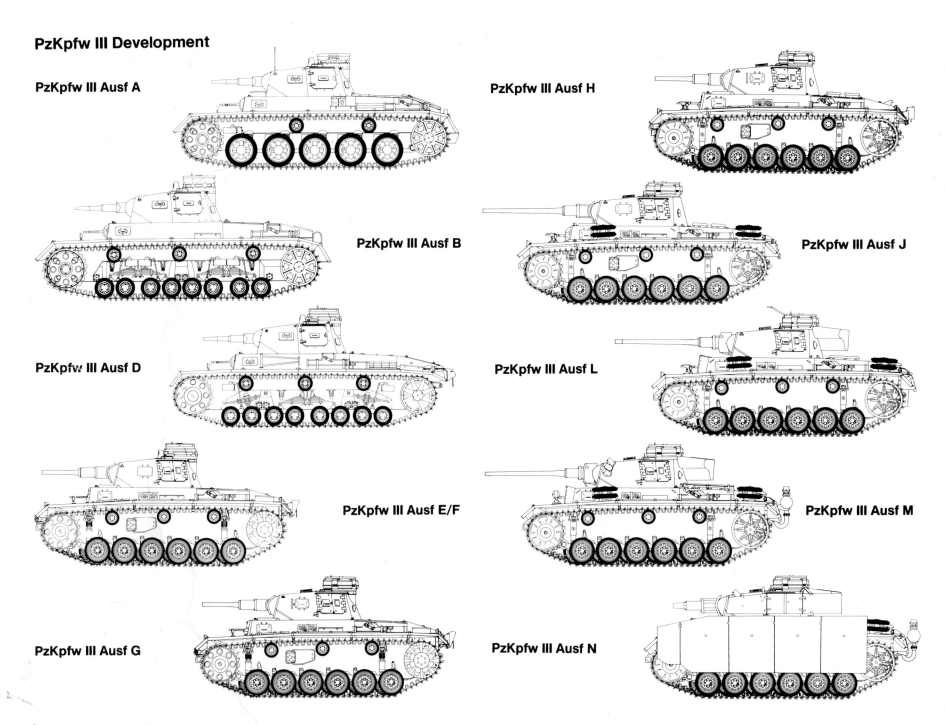

PzKpfw III Ausf A

PzKpfw III Ausf B

PzKpfw III Ausf D

PzKpfw III Ausf E/F

PzKpfw III Ausf G

PzKpfw III Ausf H

PzKpfw III Ausf J

PzKpfw III Ausf L

PzKpfw III Ausf M

PzKpfw III Ausf N

The PzKpfw III Ausf E chassis was a masterpiece of simplicity and effectiveness. The low-set drive sprocket allowed higher speeds and reduced the threat of thrown tracks, as did the adjustable large rear idler wheel. The roadwheels were mounted on pivot arms attached to transverse torsion bars mounted on the hull floor. Although the torsion bar installation did take up space in the lower hull, the better ride and ease of maintenance more than made up for the loss of interior hull stowage space.

It was a common practice to remanufacture tanks returned to the factory for major overhaul or repairs and many early models of the PzKpfw III were later re-built to the latest standards making it difficult to distinguish one variant from another. Since the improved assemblies could directly replace earlier versions, such re-building was relatively simple. This practice provided the Germans with a rapid method for replacing combat losses with up-to-date models, since tanks were usually re-built during the course of repairing or replacing battle damaged parts.

The PzKpfw III was the main battle tank of the Panzer Divisions during the early war years. Its all-round armor protection made it a better assault vehicle than the early PzKpfw IVs and many German commanders considered it a superior combat vehicle to the PzKpfw IV. During the invasion of Russia, OPERATION BARBAROSSA, the PzKpfw III fought against larger and heavier enemy tanks, such as the excellent Soviet KV-1. The short 75MM howitzers carried by the PzKpfw IV could not penetrate the armor of the KV-1, while the 50MM KwK L/42 gun on the PzKpfw III could defeat both the side and rear armor of the Soviet tank.

In North Africa, the PzKpfw III was again the most widely used German battle tank. Initially, the Germans had problems adapting the PzKpfw III for tropical service, although once these problems were solved the PzKpfw III proved to be an excellent fighting vehicle in the desert. All PzKpfw IIIs in Africa carried the 50MM L/42 (and later L/60) main gun. This weapon fired explosive-filled armor piercing projectiles and proved very effective against British armor during the early desert campaigns.

While development of the PzKpfw III paralleled that of the PzKpfw IV, the PzKpfw III had not been designed to carry heavy weapons. As the Allies introduced newer, more heavily armored and armed tanks in combat during 1942 and 1943, the effectiveness of the 50MM main armament of the PzKpfw III was greatly reduced. It later proved impossible to mount a more powerful 75MM KwK 40 long barreled gun and additional armor on the PzKpfw III to make the vehicle competitive against the newer Allied tanks.

Reluctantly, the Germans halted development of the PzKpfw III, using the chassis instead for the excellent *Sturmgeschütz* III (StuG III) assault gun. A number of PzKpfw IIIs were fitted with the short barrel 75MM L/24 howitzer used in early PzKpfw IVs as assault tanks and this successful conversion represented the heaviest weapon carried by production PzKpfw IIIs. The chassis was not capable of carrying the weight of additional armor, although the 50MM frontal armor augmented by 20MM spaced armor on the Ausf J through M was ballistically comparable to the solid 80MM armor found on later PzKpfw IVs.

Once the effectiveness of the PzKpfw III as a main battle tank had been degraded by Allied tank development, a number of vehicles were converted to command tanks while others were converted to armored munitions carriers and recovery vehicles. A number of the special command vehicles, command tanks, and other converted special purpose vehicles served in support roles until the end of the war. Additionally, in the less demanding garrison and occupation duties, such as Norway, late model PzKpfw III tanks continued to be used until the end of the war.

In addition to its role in the development of the modern main battle tank, the PzKpfw III left an even more important legacy. The torsion bar suspension, first proven on the PzKpfw III, was used in heavier versions on all later German heavy tanks until the "E" series prototypes of 1944-45. More importantly for the Allies, the British conducted a detailed technical study of a captured PzKpfw III Ausf F. Completed in 1942, this study described in detail the design and function of the superior suspension system. Copies of the report, complete with detailed technical drawings of the chassis components, were sent to the United States Army Ordnance Department for study. Two years later, the M18 Gun Motor Carriage and M24 Chaffee light tank were in production, both vehicles featuring torsion bar suspensions very similar to that of the PzKpfw III.

This same torsion bar design was also used on the T20-T26 series of medium and heavy tank prototypes. Beginning with the T26E3 (M26) Pershing heavy tank, this suspension has been widely used on light, medium, and heavy tanks for the past forty years. The torsion bar suspension was considered by many designers to be the best tank suspension available until the development of the more advanced hydropneumatic designs. The PzKpfw III had a far greater effect on the design of later tanks than most of its contemporaries; features that were introduced on it during in the mid-1930s are still in use on many of tank designs in service today.

The crew of a PzKpfw III Ausf D relaxes for a moment during the 1939 invasion of Poland. The multiple leaf suspension, cast turret cupola, and extended rear upper tailplate were features of the Ausf D. The early chassis designs of the PzKpfw III were complicated and vulnerable to enemy fire.

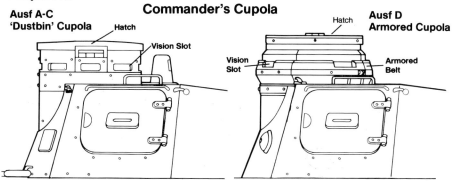

Commander's Cupola

Ausf A-C
'Dustbin' Cupola — Hatch
Vision Slot

Ausf D
Armored Cupola
Hatch
Vision Slot
Armored Belt

PANZER III AUSF E/F

The PzKpfw III Ausf E was introduced by Daimler-Benz during 1938 and was the first combat ready production model of the PzKpfw III. The major change between the Ausf E and earlier variants was the suspension. The Ausf E featured a torsion bar suspension designed by Professor Ferdinand Porsche. Professor Porsche had used the torsion bar suspension in a number of vehicles, however, the PzKpfw III represented the first successful installation of this suspension in a tank. With the introduction of the torsion bar suspension the final production configuration of the PzKpfw III was established. All further improvements to the basic design were made to update and improve the vehicle in the areas of armor protection and armament.

The use of the torsion bar suspension allowed additional armor to be carried and led to a complete redesign of the hull. Stronger single piece hull side plates replaced the earlier built up hull side plates. The torsion bars were mounted on the hull floor where they were well protected from combat damage. The vehicle's running gear was standardized at six independently sprung road wheels with three track return rollers on each side of the vehicle. This became the standard chassis for all subsequent PzKpfw III variants.

The engine was changed from the 250 hp Maybach HL 108 TR to the 300 hp Maybach HL 120 TR. The transmission was changed from a manual gearbox to the Maybach Variorex pre-selector gear box with ten forward and four reverse gears. Despite the increase in weight of the basic vehicle to more than 19 tons, the more powerful engine and improved transmission raised the top speed to 25 mph.

Armor protection was 30MM around the turret, 30MM on the front and sides of the hull and superstructure, and 16-21MM on the rear of the hull.

A number of changes were made in the equipment to improve its performance in combat. The simple flap cover on the driver's vision slot was replaced by a two-part armored visor. The single doors on the turret sides were replaced with double doors equipped with vision slots and pistol ports. Two signal ports were added to the turret roof, with the left signal port equipped with a raised armored cone which acted as a signal light shield. This armored cone was deleted on late production vehicles and was often removed during overhauls.

The follow on PzKpfw III Ausf F differed externally from the Ausf E in having armored covers on the upper hull nose for the transmission and final drive gear cooling air intakes. The engine of the Ausf F was also changed to the 300 hp Maybach HL 120 TRM, a slightly modified version of the earlier HL 120 TR.

Ausf Es and Fs were armed with the 37MM L/45 main gun, however, later remanufactured vehicles were upgunned with the 50MM L/42 cannon. The last one hundred Ausf Fs off the production line were armed with the 50MM L/42 weapon. Both vehicles were progressively modified and updated with armored air intakes being added to the Ausf E during overhaul. These updates and modifications have made it nearly impossible to distinguish between late vehicles unless the chassis number is known. Ninety-six Ausf Es

Three PzKpfw III Ausf Es of 2.PzDiv advance across open country in France during 1940. The Dark Gray lead vehicle carries the division sign consisting of two small dots in Yellow Ochre on the side and glacis and a PzRgt rhomboid and company number above the glacis division marking.

were built by Daimler-Benz, Henschel, and MAN during 1938 and 1939 with chassis numbers 60401-60496. 435 Ausf Fs were built by several manufacturers during 1939-40 with chassis numbers 61001-61650.

A PzKpfw III Ausf E advances down a dirt road in the Balkans during early 1941. The tank carries extra track links as additional protection on the front of the glacis and superstructure front plate. The Ausf E was the first variant to feature torsion bar suspension, which became a standard feature on subsequent PzKpfw III variants.

Suspension Systems

PzKpfw Ausf D
Leaf Spring
Suspension

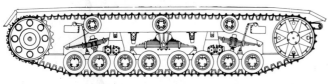

PzKpfw Ausf E
Torsion Bar
Suspension

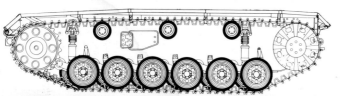

Overall Dark Gray PzKpfw III Ausf Es cross a temporary field bridge in France. The internal mantlet has two armored sleeves for the co-axial MG 34 machine guns on the starboard side of the main gun. The radio mast was hinged and could be folded down into the metal tray on the starboard side of the hull.

Driver's Vision Slot Cover

PzKpfw III Ausf D

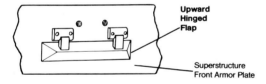

PzKpfw III Ausf E

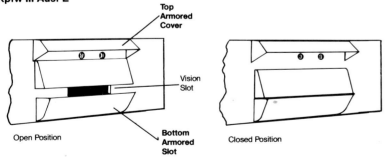

A column of PzKpfw III Ausf Es of 2.PzDiv advances along a railway in the Greek mountains during the 1941 invasion of Greece. The dusty overall Dark Gray camouflage blended well in this rocky country. The lead vehicle has dust covers fitted over the two turret co-axial machine guns.

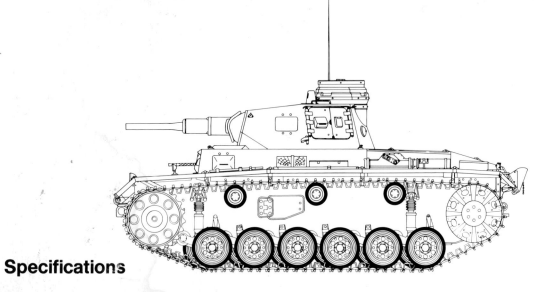

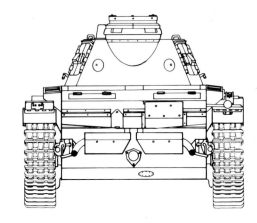

Specifications

PANZER III AUSF E/F (Late Production)

Crew	5 men
Length	17 feet 9 inches
Width	9 feet 6 inches
Height	8 feet
Weight	19.5 tons
Armament	
Main	50ᴍᴍ gun
Secondary	Three 7.92ᴍᴍ machine guns
Ammunition	131 rounds 50ᴍᴍ
	4,500 rounds 7.92ᴍᴍ
Engine	Maybach HL120TR
Horsepower	300 hp
Transmission	10 forward, 4 reverse gears
Speed	25 mph
Range	63.7 miles

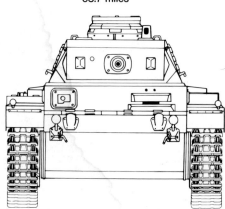

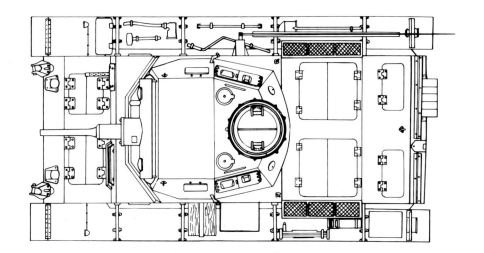

Maintenance personnel apply a fresh coat of paint to a PzKpfw III Ausf E. The vision block above the armor sleeves for the co-axial machine guns rotated upward to allow direct vision for the loader. The bolted joint between the hull and upper superstructure is visible at the front of the fender.

A PzKpfw III Ausf E has slid into a water filled shell hole and become bogged down. The screened over boxes on either side of the rear engine deck are the engine air intakes. The box on the starboard side of the tailplate houses smoke candles which could be released singly or in salvo.

Two PzKpfw IVs attempt to tow a bogged down PzKpfw III Ausf E out of a muddy shell hole. The Pzkpfw IV on the left has the rear fender mud guards raised to prevent them from becoming caked with mud thrown up by the tracks and possibly fouling the idler wheel.

11

A PzKpfw III Ausf E of 5.PzDiv rolls past a group of infantrymen during the invasion of the Low Countries. The tank is overall Dark Gray with the division sign in Yellow Ochre. The Notek blackout driving light has been moved from its usual position on the port mudguard to the front of the glacis next to the port headlight.

A PzKpfw III Ausf E prepares to ford a steam in the Balkans during 1941. The single door turret hatch cover of the Ausf D was replaced by double doors on the Ausf E. The side hull escape hatch located between the first two return rollers was the fastest exit for the driver and radio operator since the PzKpfw III lacked crew hatches in the superstructure top plate.

A PzKpfw III Ausf E of 13.PzDiv (background) has pulled alongside a *Panzerbefehlswagen* III Ausf H (PzBefWg III) on the Russian steppes during OPERATION BARBAROSSA, the 1941 invasion of Russia. The PzBefWg III was a command tank variant of the PzKpfw III fitted with extensive radio equipment.

Turret Side Hatch

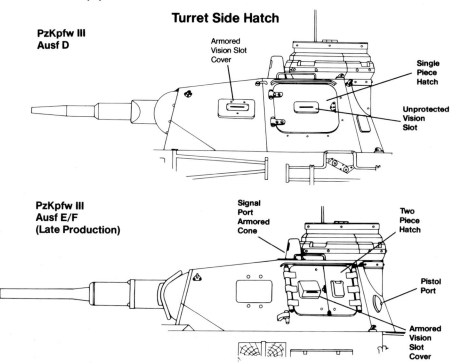

PzKpfw III
Ausf D

Armored Vision Slot Cover

Single Piece Hatch

Unprotected Vision Slot

PzKpfw III
Ausf E/F
(Late Production)

Signal Port Armored Cone

Two Piece Hatch

Pistol Port

Armored Vision Slot Cover

A very dusty overall Dark Gray PzKpfw III Ausf E or F passes infantrymen on a road in the Balkans during 1941. The signal light cover over the left turret roof signal port is in place, however, during maintenance this cover was often removed. A heavy coat of dust has nearly obscured the tank's markings, except for the lion painted on the cupola.

A PzKpfw III Ausf F is prepared for shipment by railcar in France during mid-1941. The tank is overall Dark Gray, with a heavy coating of dust and mud on the chassis. The PzKpfw II Ausf C on the rear flatcar is believed to be painted in Desert Yellow.

A crewman bail
sian stream. Th
30мм armor pla

A reworked PzK
The armor plate
piercing cap of
armor plate ben

A crewman cleans the 37мм main gun of a Pz
tinguished from the nearly identical Ausf E
intakes on the glacis (one of these covers i

Air I

PzKpfw III Ausf F/Rebuilt E

Armor

14

The last 100 PzKpfw III Ausf Fs were up-gunned with the 50мм KwK L/42 cannon during production and the majority of older vehicles were retro-fitted with this weapon during factory overhauls. The roadwheels hung on the extra track on the glacis served as spaced armor to help break up armor-piercing projectiles.

s water out of a PzKpfw III Ausf F of 1.PzDiv that has become mired in a Rus-
tank is armed with the 50мм KwK L/42 gun in an external mantlet and has
added to both the hull and superstructure front.

pfw III Ausf F of 10.PzDiv kicks up a cloud of dust on the dry Russian plain.
installed on the front of the superstructure stripped off the external armor-
an anti-tank round, causing the shot to break up on impact with the main
ath.

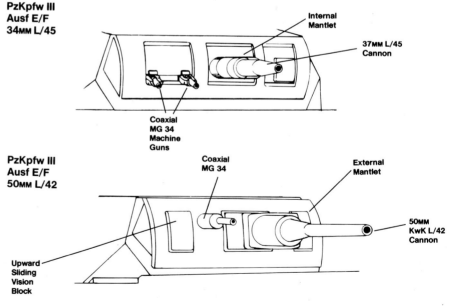

PzKpfw III Ausf E/F 34мм L/45

Internal Mantlet

37мм L/45 Cannon

Coaxial MG 34 Machine Guns

PzKpfw III Ausf E/F 50мм L/42

Coaxial MG 34

External Mantlet

50мм KwK L/42 Cannon

Upward Sliding Vision Block

PANZER III AUSF G

The PzKpfw III Ausf G was a further development of the PzKpfw III Ausf F with the major structural change being an increase in the rear hull armor protection from 21 to 30MM. Additionally, the vertically sliding armored block on the driver's vision port was replaced with an armored pivoting cover. A number of late production vehicles were fitted with wider 400MM tracks, however, the majority of Ausf Gs were built with the standard 360MM tracks.

The turret of the Ausf G was altered with the left signal port on the turret roof being deleted. The first fifty Ausf Gs off the production line were armed with the 37MM L/45 main gun with the remainder being armed with the 50MM KwK L/42 cannon. The L/42 gun was mounted in an external mantlet with two vision blocks and a co-axial MG 34 machine gun on the starboard side of the main gun. By the end of 1942 most early production Ausf Gs had been retro-fitted with the 50MM gun.

The Ausf G was the first PzKpfw III variant to be equipped with a turret ventilator fan. The fan on early production Ausf Gs was mounted on the turret roof directly in front of the commander's cupola, which proved to be an unsatisfactory location. After further testing the fan's position was standardized for production with the fan being mounted in the middle of the turret roof offset slightly to starboard. Late in the production run, a new cast cupola with better armor protection was introduced. This cupola had the earlier segmented sliding armored covers over the vision slots replaced by twin covers that opened vertically. The new cupola was identical to the cupola fitted to the late PzKpfw IV.

Vehicles intended for tropical use were modified with additional air filters and a modified cooling fan gear ratio. After modification these vehicles were re-designated PzKpfw III Ausf G(Tp) (Tp for tropical).

Some 600 PzKpfw III Ausf Gs were produced during 1940-41. Chassis numbers were 65001-65950, although the blocks of numbers assigned were usually larger than the actual number of vehicles produced (for security reasons). In common with earlier variants, many Ausf Gs were later rebuilt and brought up to later standards.

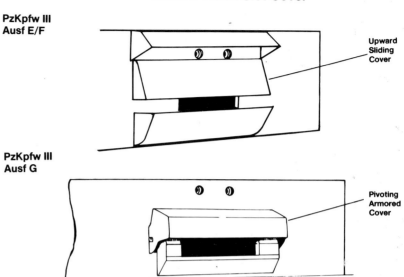

Driver's Vision Slot Cover

PzKpfw III Ausf E/F

Upward Sliding Cover

PzKpfw III Ausf G

Pivoting Armored Cover

German infantry take cover behind a line of PzKpfw IIIs in Russia during 1941. The tank on the right is a PzKpfw III Ausf G which featured a re-designed cupola identical to the one fitted on late production PzKpfw IVs.

A PzKpfw III Ausf G fords a stream in Greece during late 1941. The chassis number "65940" on the superstructure side indicates that this was one of the last Ausf G's built. The overall Dark Gray camouflage is broken only by the White chassis number, diamond playing card symbol, and the Yellow Ochre 2.PzDiv sign on the superstructure plate.

Turret

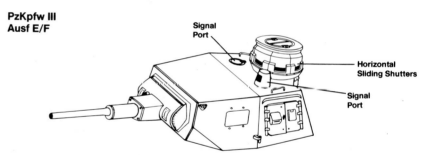

PzKpfw III Ausf E/F

- Signal Port
- Horizontal Sliding Shutters
- Signal Port

(Above) An overall Dark Gray PzKpfw III Ausf G of PzRgt 31, 5.PzDiv passes a burning building during the invasion of Russia. The turret stowage box on the back of the turret became a standard feature on later variants and was often retrofitted to earlier models.

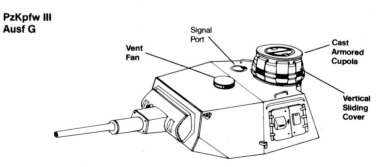

PzKpfw III Ausf G

- Vent Fan
- Signal Port
- Cast Armored Cupola
- Vertical Sliding Cover

(Left) A mid-production PzKpfw III Ausf G advances across open country in the Balkans. As was common, the unit work shop (or possibly the crew) has installed a frame to hold extra equipment on the rear deck. The thick dust has almost obscured the German national flag carried on the rear deck to identify the tank as friendly to *Luftwaffe* aircraft.

An overall Dark Gray PzKpfw III Ausf G of PzRgt 5, 5.LtDiv, *Deutsches Afrikakorps* (DAK) is off loaded in Tripoli harbor. The turret number is Red outlined in White. The air vent covers on the engine access hatches were developed for the tropicalized tanks used by the DAK in Africa.

(Below) This PzKpfw III Ausf G of the 1st company, PzRgt 8, 15.PzDiv has the wider 40mm tracks first fitted to late production Ausf Gs. The vehicle is overall Yellow Brown desert camouflage with the turret number in Red outlined in White.

(Above) A tropicalized PzKpfw III Ausf G is lowered to the dock after being off loaded from a German freighter in Tripoli. The stowage racks for carrying water filled jerrycans were fitted to tanks of PzRgt 5 for operations in the desert.

PANZER III *TAUCHPANZER*

The PzKpfw III *Tauchpanzer* was a submersible wading tank designed for OPERA-TION SEA LION, the planned invasion of England. A total of 168 vehicles were converted from PzKpfw III Ausf Fs (37MM and 50MM), PzKpfw III Ausf Gs, PzKpfw III Ausf Hs, and a number of PzBefWg III command tanks. The conversion program was completed by late fall of 1940 with the vehicles being assigned to *Panzerabteilung* A, a special unit formed at Putlos in northern Germany.

The *Tauchpanzer* was intended to operate in water up to 15 meters (49.2 feet) deep, approaching the invasion beaches underwater after being launched offshore from special transport barges. The tanks were made watertight with all openings being sealed with either sealing compound or waterproof fabric covers. The engine air intakes were sealed with locking covers and the exhaust system was modified with one-way valves. An inflatable rubber tube was installed in the joint between the hull and turret that, when inflated, sealed the turret ring creating a watertight joint. The guns were covered with watertight rubber covers that had detonating cord imbedded in the covers. After landing these covers could be blown off the guns from within the tank.

To supply air to the vehicle, a fifty foot flexible snorkel tube was mounted at the rear of the tank. The snorkel was supported by a float which also carried a radio antenna for communications. A pump was installed to remove any sea water that might seep into the tank and a gyrocompass was carried for navigation to the shore.

The cancellation of OPERATION SEA LION eliminated the need for these extensively modified vehicles and during the spring of 1941 most were further modified for use in river crossings. The waterproofing equipment was simplified with the long flexible snorkel being replaced by a ten foot steel tube extending up from the commander's cupola. These modified *Tauchpanzer* wading tanks were issued to 18.PzDiv and PzReg 6 of 3.PzDiv. During OPERATION BARBAROSSA, the invasion of Russia, wading tanks of the 18.PzDiv conducted a crossed the Bug River. After crossing the river the wading PzKpfw IIIs were used as standard combat tanks.

A crane lifts a *Tauchpanzer* III submersible tank out over the water, while high ranking German officers look on. *Tauchpanzer* IIIs were converted PzKpfw III Ausf Fs armed with the 37MM cannon. The covers on the engine deck and guns were of waterproof fabric with waterproof rubber seals used around the doors and vision ports in the turret.

High ranking German officials inspect a *Tauchpanzer* being prepared for a test run during late 1940. The fifty foot flexible snorkel hose fed air into the tank and was supported on the water's surface by a special float which also carried a radio antenna for communications.

A crewman provides covering fire while a second crewman exits the hull escape hatch of a PzKpfw III wading tank of PzRgt 6, 3.PzDiv while on temporary assignment to 4.PzDiv for training. The wading tank had an inflatable rubber turret ring seal and extended plates on the superstructure that sealed the turret ring in any traverse position.

PzKpfw III wading tanks could ford water up to 3 feet deep without special preparations because of the extended rear engine exhaust stacks. This early production PzKpfw III Ausf G wading tank has an early style cupola.

Gun Cover Frames

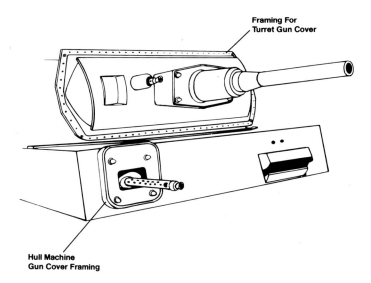

Framing For
Turret Gun Cover

Hull Machine
Gun Cover Framing

When the invasion of England (OPERATION SEA LION) was cancelled the majority of *Tauchpanzer* III's were modified as wading tanks. This wading tank is attached to 4.PzDiv for training. The frame around the turret front was the mounting frame for the gun mantlet waterproof fabric cover.

A PzKpfw III Ausf G wading tank with the engine side air intakes raised to improve engine cooling. These waterproof covers could be released from inside the vehicle once it was on dry land. '213' is overall Dark Gray with Yellow Ochre turret numbers. The bear on the turret side is Red with a White border.

(Below) German infantry moves up alongside a PzKpfw III Ausf G wading tank of 18.PzDiv, the primary user of PzKpfw III wading tanks. '631' is an early Ausf G retro-fitted with the revised cupola. The metal frames around the mantlet and hull MG mount distinguish this vehicle from standard battle tanks.

(Above) A pair of PzKpfw III wading tanks during training in preparation for the invasion of Russia. The extended rear exhaust pipes were later adopted for use on the PzKpfw III Ausf M as standard equipment.

PANZER III AUSF H

Combat experience in both Poland and France led to a realization that the PzKpfw III was under armored. While work was initiated on an up-armored variant, an interim model with applique armor, improved suspension, and a new transmission was introduced under the designation PzKpfw III Ausf H.

The basic interior armor configuration was unaltered, however, the Ausf H was modified with applique 30MM armor plates welded to the exterior of the hull rear, and front of both hull and superstructure, giving the Ausf H a total of 60MM of armor in critical areas. This added armor protection was sufficient to defeat the standard tank guns of 1941, as well as most anti-tank guns then in service.

The complex Variorex pre-selective type transmission (ten forward and four reverse gears) was replaced with a Maybach synchromech transmission with six forward gears and one reverse gear. To lower the vehicle's ground pressure, the Ausf H was fitted with a re-designed 400MM wide track which accommodated the increase in the vehicle's weight brought about by the added armor without increasing the ground pressure. A new drive sprocket and rear idler were designed, however, these were not standardized until later and the majority of Ausf H tanks were built with the original idlers and drive sprockets modified with a 40MM spacer ring to accept the new track. The modified sprocket and idler assemblies were interchangeable with the new design units and a number of repaired vehicles have been noted with one type of drive sprocket on one side of the vehicle and the other type on the opposite side. The first track return roller on each side of the vehicle was repositioned slightly forward to prevent the heavier track from sagging and fouling the front shock absorber strut.

The turret was redesigned to relieve the cramped conditions that resulted from installation of the 50MM cannon. The rear turret armor plate was replaced with a single 30MM plate that eliminated the cut out for the cupola. This provided more room inside the turret to clear the recoil stroke of the 50MM gun, and gave better protection to the base of the cupola. The turret was also modified with a rotating turret basket, which allowed the crew to stand on the basket floor and turn with the turret. This feature was eventually retro-fitted to earlier PzKpfw III models when the vehicles were returned to the factory for up-gunning with the 50MM cannon.

The development of the PzKpfw III Ausf J which incorporated all of these improvements as part of the tank's basic design led to a reduction in production orders for the Ausf H with 408 being built between late 1940 and the Spring of 1941 (chassis numbers 66001-66650).

Crewmen work to free a bogged down PzKpfw III Ausf H of 1.PzDiv on a dirt road in Russia during early 1942. The superstructure front carries applique armor plate with cutouts for the driver's visor and hull MG mount. This vehicle is painted in the African camouflage scheme of Yellow Brown.

Front Superstructure Applique Armor

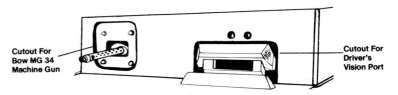

Cutout For Bow MG 34 Machine Gun

Cutout For Driver's Vision Port

A PzKpfw III Ausf H of PzRgt 5, 21.PzDiv (formerly 5.LtDiv) advances across the desert near Marmarika, Libya in December of 1941. PzRgt 5 equipped most of its vehicles with external stowage racks for fuel and water jerry cans. The extra track links on the hull and superstructure front were for added protection against armor piercing anti-tank rounds.

Suspension System

PzKpfw III Ausf G

360MM Track

PzKpfw III Ausf H

Repositioned Track Return Roller

Revised Idler

Revised Drive Sprocket

400MM Track

This late production PzKpfw III Ausf H of 1.PzDiv has the revised drive sprocket and rear idler installed for use with the 400mm track. This vehicle has been fitted with a non-standard rectangular turret stowage box which is larger than the standard production box.

An overall Dark Gray PzKpfw III Ausf H crosses a temporary bridge across a stream in Russia. The turret stowage box is the standard production version with cutaway sides to clear the rear turret pistol ports. The turret numbers are Red outlined in White.

A PzKpfw III Ausf H, hit on a Russian road during June of 1942, has been set afire and its ammunition is cooking off. The chassis is the early production version with the 360mm track and early style drive sprocket, idler wheel, and return roller locations.

Rear Turret Armor Plate

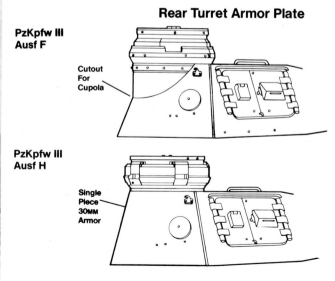

PzKpfw III Ausf F

Cutout For Cupola

PzKpfw III Ausf H

Single Piece 30mm Armor

PANZER III AUSF J

The PzKpfw III Ausf J was the first variant to feature 50MM integral front and rear armor and was the last basic model of the PzKpfw III produced. Subsequent variants were modifications of the Ausf J optimized for greater simplicity or effectiveness. While the hull and superstructure front and rear armor plate had been increased to 50MM thick, the side armor remained the basic 30MM thickness. The hull side plates were extended in front of the hull nose to form towing eyes for tow cables. The turret armor remained 30MM all around, however, the gun mantlet armor was increased to 50MM.

The increase in armor required a number of changes to the hull. The driver's visor was modified and the hull MG mount was now reconfigured with a pronounced ball mount that extended ahead of the front armor plate (these fittings were identical to those used on the PzKpfw IV Ausf F). The two piece equipment access hatches on the glacis were replaced with single piece access hatches and the armored air intake covers for the transmission and final drive units were revised. To improve protection for the smoke candle installation, it was repositioned under the rear engine compartment tailplate.

With the introduction of the Ausf J the 400MM track with revised drive sprockets and rear idlers were standardized and all Ausf Js were built with these features as standard equipment. A number of repaired vehicles, however, have been noted with the Ausf H style drive sprockets or idlers installed. These parts were interchangable and were used whenever there were shortages of the proper repair parts. Late in the production run, 20MM spaced armor was added to the superstructure front and (less often) gun mantlet. The spaced armor was effective in defeating anti-tank shells by stripping off the shell's armor piercing nose cap, causing the shot to break up upon hitting the main armor plate beneath the spaced armor.

Early production Ausf Js were armed with the 50MM KwK L/42 gun. In August 1940, however, Hitler insisted on up-gunning the PzKpfw III with a more powerful weapon. The German Ordnance Department did not immediately comply with Hitler's wishes since the 50MM L/42 gun, first introduced in mid-1940, had proven to be an effective weapon in combat. In April 1941, Hitler again inspected the PzKpfw III Ausf J and insisted that the L/42 gun be replaced with the long barreled 50MM L/60 gun.

In December of 1941 the L/60 was introduced onto the production line as standard equipment on the Ausf J. Besides the changes in the gun and mount, the internal ammunition stowage was reduced from ninety-nine to eighty-four rounds because of the larger size of the L/60's shell casings. The appearance of the Soviet T-34 and KV-1 tanks in Russia soon proved the wisdom of a heavier weapon. The L/60 gun proved to be effective against British and American tanks during combat in North Africa, however, the weapon was less effective against the better armored Russian T-34 and KV-1.

The Ausf J was built by several manufacturers between early 1941 and mid-1942 with a total of 1549 short-barreled L/42 armed Ausf Js and 1067 long-barreled L/60 armed Ausf Js being produced (chassis numbers 68001-69000 and 72001-74100). The *Sonderkraftfahrzeug* (special vehicle number — SdKfz) number of the L/60 armed vehicles was changed to SdKfz 141/1, denoting the different gun.

(Right) A PzKpfw III Ausf J climbs a muddy grade, throwing back water and mud from its tracks. The Ausf J chassis had the main tailplate as part of the lower hull and the narrow upper tailpiece as part of the engine compartment assembly. The sheet metal flap below the main tailplate is a deflector to reduce dust thrown up by the engine exhaust.

A PzKpfw III Ausf J ploughs through a muddy field during maneuvers in Germany. The revised driver's visor and hull machine gun mount were used on both the PzKpfw III and IV. The Ausf J featured revised glacis hatches, air intake covers, and towing eyes.

Superstructure Front Plate

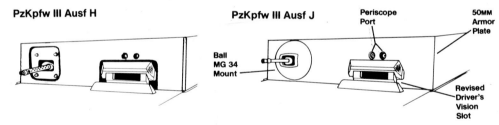

PzKpfw III Ausf H

PzKpfw III Ausf J

Periscope Port

50MM Armor Plate

Ball MG 34 Mount

Revised Driver's Vision Slot

This captured PzKpfw III Ausf J of 21.PzDiv (DAK) was returned to England for evaluation. Tropical engine deck air Intakes were installed on the hinged engine access hatches. These intakes could be easily retro-fitted to earlier variants by replacing the access hatches with new hatches and air intakes.

A column of overall Dark Gray PzKpfw III Ausf Js of 4.PzDiv advances through a Russian town during 1941-42. Because of a shortage of transport and the poor off-road performance of most German military trucks it was common for tanks traveling toward the front to carry extra fuel and oil in drums or jerry cans.

The crews of these overall Dark Gray PzKpfw III Ausf Js of 24.PzDiv wait for the order to attack during the fighting in Russia. The tank in the center carries the official division sign, a Yellow Ochre upward slanting arrow on the superstructure front while the leaping horse and rider of the old 1.Cavalry Division is carried in White on the mudguard.

Air Intake Covers

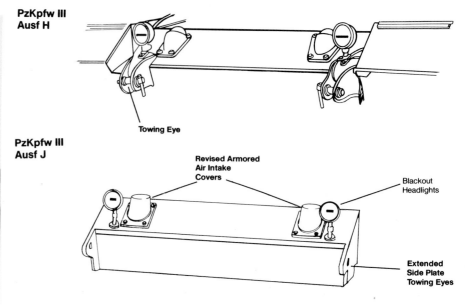

PzKpfw III
Ausf H

Towing Eye

PzKpfw III
Ausf J

Revised Armored
Air Intake
Covers

Blackout
Headlights

Extended
Side Plate
Towing Eyes

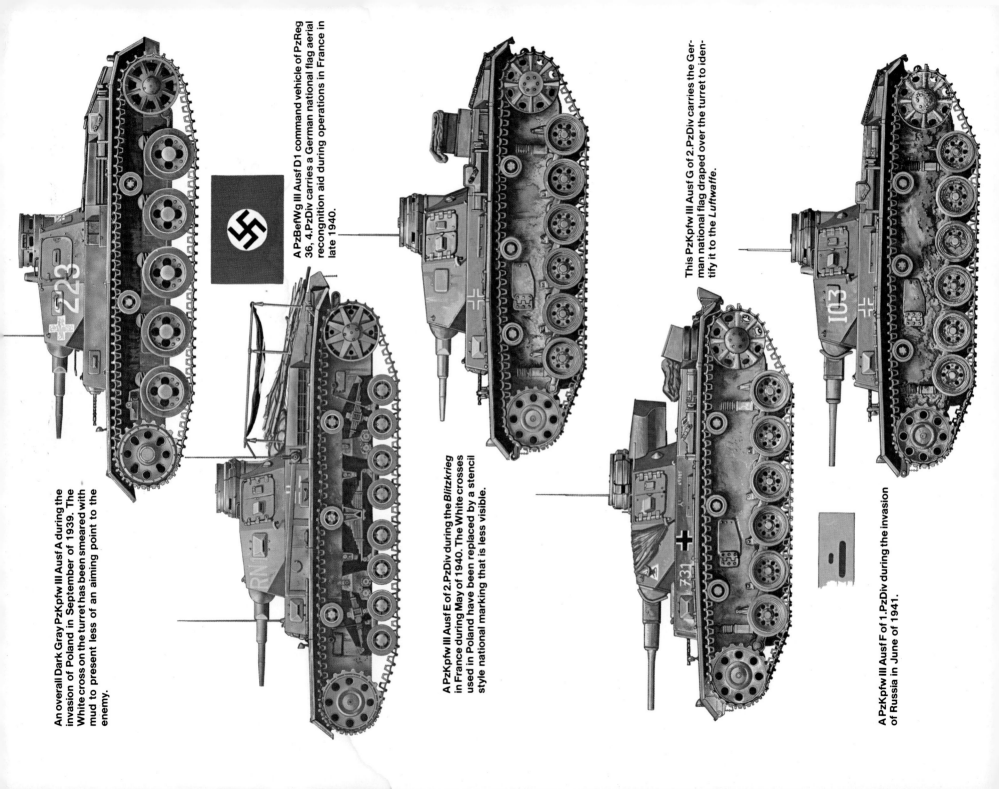

An overall Dark Gray PzKpfw III Ausf A during the invasion of Poland in September of 1939. The White cross on the turret has been smeared with mud to present less of an aiming point to the enemy.

A PzBefWg III Ausf D1 command vehicle of PzReg 36, 4.PzDiv carries a German national flag aerial recongnition aid during operations in France in late 1940.

This PzKpfw III Ausf G of 2.PzDiv carries the German national flag draped over the turret to identify it to the Luftwaffe.

A PzKpfw III Ausf E of 2.PzDiv during the Blitzkrieg in France during May of 1940. The White crosses used in Poland have been replaced by a stencil style national marking that is less visible.

A PzKpfw III Ausf F of 1.PzDiv during the invasion of Russia in June of 1941.

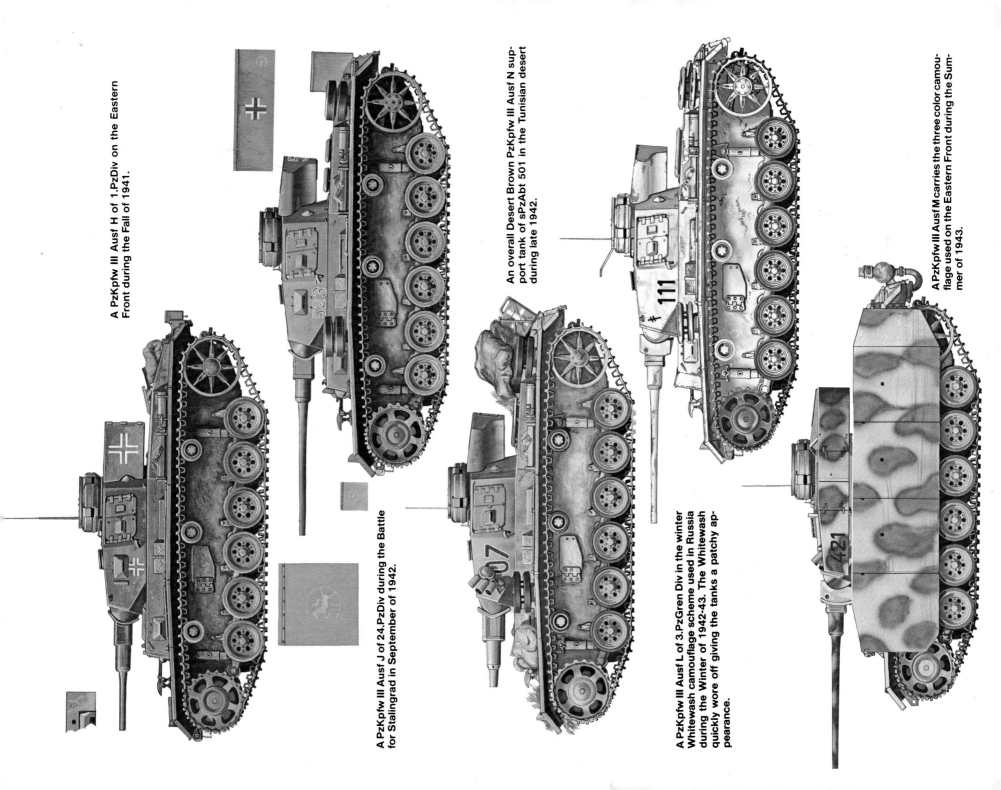

A PzKpfw III Ausf H of 1.PzDiv on the Eastern Front during the Fall of 1941.

A PzKpfw III Ausf J of 24.PzDiv during the Battle for Stalingrad in September of 1942.

An overall Desert Brown PzKpfw III Ausf N support tank of sPzAbt 501 in the Tunisian desert during late 1942.

A PzKpfw III Ausf L of 3.PzGren Div in the winter Whitewash camouflage scheme used in Russia during the Winter of 1942-43. The Whitewash quickly wore off giving the tanks a patchy appearance.

A PzKpfw III Ausf M carries the three color camouflage used on the Eastern Front during the Summer of 1943.

PzKpfw III Ausf Js of 2.PzDiv advance past a line of SdKfz 10 one ton artillery tractors on a dirt road in Russia during the Summer of 1941. The vehicles are overall Dark Gray, with the unit and tactical markings in White.

This PzKpfw III Ausf J of PzRgt 31, 5.PzDiv is Dark Gray overpainted with temporary winter Whitewash camouflage. The Whitewash wore off quickly giving the tank a patchy appearance. The PzRgt 31 insignia, a Red devil, is stencilled on the side of the turret in front of the vision port.

5.PzDiv was originally intended to reinforce Rommel in North Africa, however, heavy losses in Russia required that additional units be quickly sent to the Eastern Front. 5.PzDiv deployed to Russia with many of its tanks painted in the Yellow Brown camouflage used in Africa.

An overall Africa Yellow Brown PzKpfw III Ausf J of 5.PzDiv churns through a muddy field in Russia during 1942. The patches around the turret markings are Dark Gray. The crew has modified this vehicle with a field built stowage rack across the tailplate.

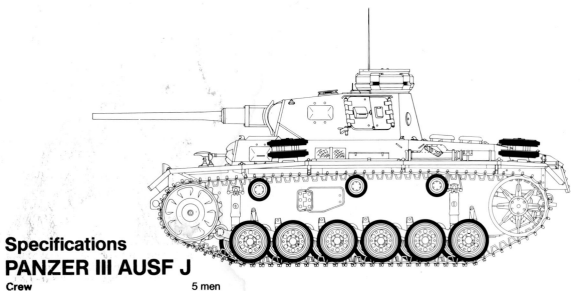

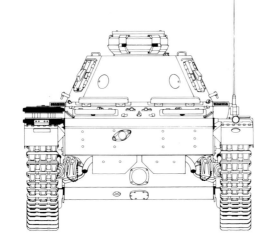

Specifications
PANZER III AUSF J

Crew	5 men
Length	18 feet
Width	9 feet 7 inches
Height	8 feet 3 inches
Weight	19.5 tons
Armarment	
Main	50ᴍᴍ L/42 gun or
	50ᴍᴍ L/60 gun
Secondary	Two 7.92ᴍᴍ machine guns
Ammunition	99 rounds 50ᴍᴍ
	3,750 rounds 7.92ᴍᴍ
Engine	Maybach HL120TRM
Horsepower	300 hp
Transmission	10 forward, 1 reverse gear
Speed	25 mph
Range	59.8 miles

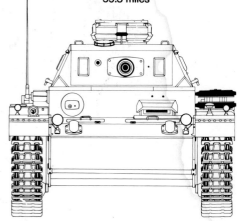

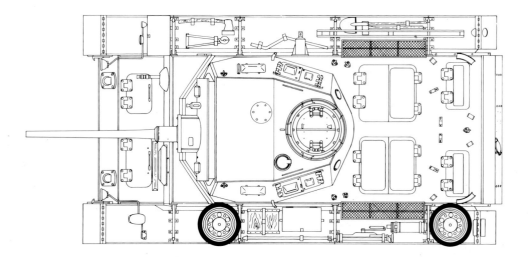

This snow camouflaged PzKpfw III Ausf J has the port vision flap on the mantlet open and has dust covers on all the weapons. The White temporary camouflage was washable and quickly wore off in action.

A PzKpfw III Ausf J of 23.PzDiv passes through a Russian village behind the lines. Dust covers have been installed on all the tank's guns to protect them from dirt and dust. The crew has added two layers of spare track to the hull front for extra protection from anti-tank rounds.

PzKpfw III Ausf Js of 24.PzDiv advance across open country during the battle of Stalingrad in the Winter of 1942-43. Originally in Dark Gray (left) or Dark Yellow (center) these tanks are camouflaged with Whitewash on all vertical surfaces. Shortages of Whitewash often led to painting only those surfaces which could be seen from ground level.

This burned out PzKpfw III Ausf J has been fitted with the wide *Ostketten* tracks developed for the Russian front to give better traction in mud and snow. The spare track links on the hull front are held in place by welded racks which became common on most PzKpfw IIIs and IVs.

PzKpfw III Ausf Js of 23.PzDiv move across Russian fields in the spring of 1943. These tanks mount the long barreled 50mm KwK39 L/60 gun and are painted in Dark Yellow. The Eiffel Tower division sign is carried on the starboard fender in White.

A PzKpfw III Ausf J passes a snow mobile being towed by a horse near the village of Smolensk in Russia during the Winter of 1941-42. A well applied snow camouflage paint scheme was effective in concealing the tank against the snow covered landscape.

PzKpfw III Ausf J Main Armament

**Short Barrel
50mm KwK
L/42 Cannon**

**Long Barrel
50mm KwK 39
L/60 Cannon**

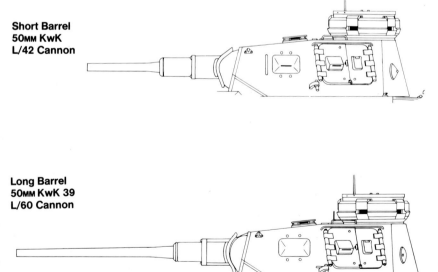

An overall Dark Yellow PzKpfw III Ausf J crosses an open field in Russia during 1941/42. The small turret number '322', partially obscured by water bottles strung on the turret side, is in Black. The long barreled L/60 gun increased the overall length of the vehicle by 2.46 feet.

PzKpfw III Ausf Js of 24.PzDiv advance toward Stalingrad. The crew has added extra track links to the turret roof as well as the superstructure and hull front. The division sign on the starboard fender and the outline Panzer unit rhomboid tactical sign on the gun recoil tube are in White.

Crewmen of 24.PzDiv ease a PzKpfw III Ausf J off a flatcar prior to beginning the Stalingrad campaign. The vehicle is overall dusty Dark Gray, with the 1.Cavalry Division sign in White on the starboard fender. This vehicle is armed with the L/60 gun and has stowage boxes fitted on the fenders.

Late production PzKpfw III Ausf Js, and rebuilt earlier variants, were fitted with thin armor skirts for protection against shaped charge projectiles. This Ausf J of 20.PzDiv in Russia is camouflaged in Dark Yellow over-sprayed with broad areas of Olive Green with the division sign in Yellow Ochre against a patch of the Dark Gray.

A number of PzKpfw III gun tanks were converted to command tanks to supplement the limited numbers of production command vehicles. This converted PzKpfw III Ausf J has rails on the hull for armor skirts and a star rod antenna that replaced the large frame antennas carried by command tanks.

This PzKpfw III Ausf J, believed to be of 1.PzDiv is fitted with a non-standard turret stowage bin similar to those seen on earlier PzKpfw III Ausf Hs. The Dark Gray camouflage has been overpainted with a hand brushed pattern of Dark Yellow.

PANZER III AUSF L

In early 1942, the German Army Ordnance Department began a study to determine the possibility of mounting the turret of the PzKpfw IV, with its 75MM KwK40 gun, on the chassis of the PzKpfw III. The study showed that numerous modifications would be necessary to mount the turret on the PzKpfw III chassis and it was doubtful that the chassis could handle the additional weight. Since these modifications would have disrupted production of badly needed tanks, the Ordnance Department's final report recommended abandoning the project and continuing production of the PzKpfw III armed with the KwK39 L/60 gun with modifications to improve the turret gun mount.

These modifications were tested on a PzKpfw III Ausf J and standardized for production with the new variant being designated PzKpfw III Ausf L. The turret front armor plate was increased to 57MM and the coil spring gun recoil mechanism was replaced with a torsion bar gun counter balance. The addition of the gun counter-balance reduced ammunition stowage from eighty-four to seventy-eight rounds. The engine deck access hatches were redesigned as one piece units hinged at the front and the air intakes were repositioned fore-and-aft rather than transversely. Large air intake covers were mounted on the two rear engine access hatches.

The Ausf L was the first PzKpfw III variant to use spaced armor. The use of spaced armor involves mounting armor plates slightly ahead of the main armor with an air space between the two. The explosive effect of high explosive rounds is somewhat dissipated by this type of armor. The Ausf L had 20MM spaced armor added to the superstructure front plate and gun mantlet. In an effort to reduce production time and conserve resources, a number of items were deleted from the vehicle including the hull side escape hatches, the loader's vision port in the mantlet, and turret side vision ports.

Originally, 1100 Ausf Ls were ordered, however, only 653 (chassis numbers 74101-75500) were actually produced. In mid-1942, nearly half of the Ausf L order was cancelled to allow production of a new variant mounting the 75MM L/24 howitzer.

German infantry catch a ride on the back of a PzKpfw III Ausf L as it passes through a Russian town during the Spring of 1943. The large national flag on the rear deck was used as an aerial recognition aid. This tank is painted overall Dark Yellow, the turret numbers are in Red and the tactical signs on the tailplate are in White.

PzKpfw III Ausf Ls drive down a stone street in a Russian village during late 1942. The support frame on the gun mantlet is for spaced 20MM armor which was designed to defeat armor piercing anti-tank rounds. This vehicle is overall Dark Yellow with White turret numbers.

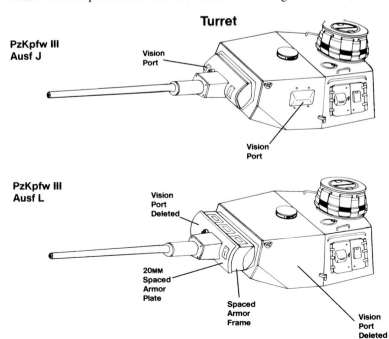

Turret

PzKpfw III Ausf J

Vision Port

Vision Port

PzKpfw III Ausf L

Vision Port Deleted

20MM Spaced Armor Plate

Spaced Armor Frame

Vision Port Deleted

A late production overall Dark Yellow PzKpfw III Ausf L is ferried across a Russian river during the Summer of 1943. The turret side vision ports, loader's mantlet vision port, and hull side escape hatches were deleted on the Ausf L to cut production time.

A column of late production PzKpfw III Ausf Ls advance through a town in southern France. The cutout in the left rear mudguard was to allow installation of a Notek blackout tail light.

A crewman cleans the long barreled 50мм L/60 gun of a PzKpfw III Ausf L outside a Russian hut during the Spring of 1943. The 20мм spaced armor was bolted to a subframe attached to the mantlet which kept the armor at the proper distance from the mantlet for maximum protection.

The SdKfz 9 eighteen ton tractor and tank transporter trailer were widely used to carry vehicles between the front and maintenance facilities. The PzKpfw III Ausf L of PzDiv *Hermann Goering* is painted in a Dark Yellow pattern over a Dark Gray base, with the turret numbers in Red outlined in White.

German maintenance crews use a mobile crane to lift the turret off a PzKpfw III Ausf L at a forward repair depot in Russia. The turret basket was removed before the turret was taken off. Because of its bolted-together sub-assemblies, the PzKpfw III could be easily repaired in the field.

Superstructure Spaced Armor

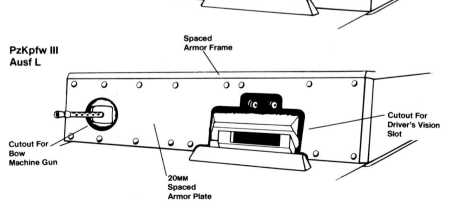

PzKpfw III
Ausf J

PzKpfw III
Ausf L

Spaced
Armor Frame

Cutout For
Driver's Vision
Slot

Cutout For
Bow
Machine Gun

20MM
Spaced
Armor Plate

Although badly damaged tanks were usually sent to overhaul depots for major repairs, it was not uncommon for field repair shops to rebuild as many vehicles as possible. Sub-assemblies could be exchanged between tanks allowing parts from seriously damaged tanks to be easily salvaged for use in repairing other vehicles.

After removing the turret, the superstructure could be easily unbolted from the hull and lifted off. With the superstructure removed maintenance crews could easily reach the transmission, drive train and final drive units for repair or overhaul.

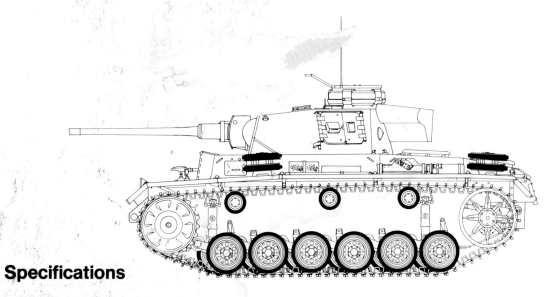

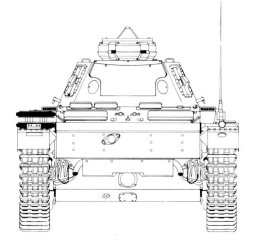

Specifications

PANZER III AUSF L

Crew	5 men
Length	18 feet 3 inches
Width	9 feet 7 inches
Height	8 feet 3 inches
Weight	23.1 tons
Armarment	
Main	50мм L/60 gun
Secondary	Two 7.92мм machine guns
Ammunition	78 rounds 50мм
	4,950 rounds 7.92мм
Engine	Maybach HL120TRM
Horsepower	300 hp
Transmission	10 forward, 1 reverse gear
Speed	25 mph
Range	59.8 miles

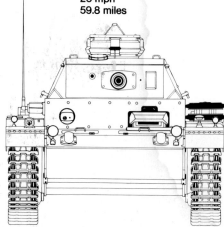

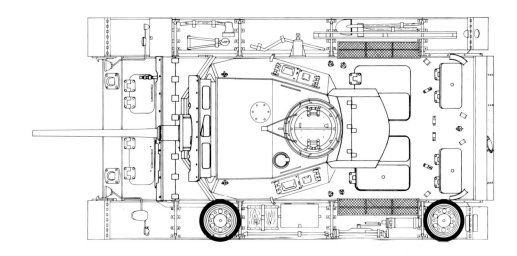

This early production Ausf L is equipped with *Ostketten* extended tracks. These tracks were easily damaged as is evidenced by the bent and broken track extensions. The badly worn snow camouflage is compromised by the extensive external stowage on the rear deck.

Hull Escape Hatch

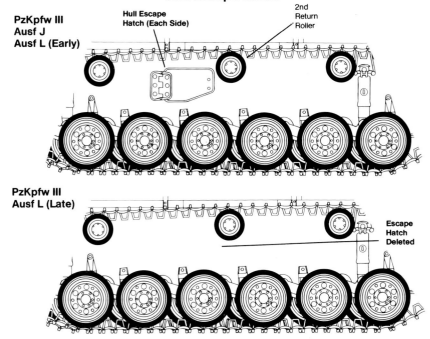

PzKpfw III
Ausf J
Ausf L (Early)

Hull Escape
Hatch (Each Side)

2nd
Return
Roller

PzKpfw III
Ausf L (Late)

Escape
Hatch
Deleted

Crewmen work to replace the damaged drive sprocket of a snow camouflaged PzKpfw III Ausf L of 3.PzGrenDiv. The replacement drive sprocket is Dark Gray and the turret numbers and division sign are in Black. The frame on the mantlet is for 20mm spaced armor.

10th PzDiv formed a major part of the German forces in Tunisia during 1942 and 1943. This PzKpfw III Ausf L shows the typical appearance of 10.PzDiv's PzKpfw IIIs. The vehicle is overall Dark Yellow with the company number in Dark Red and a thick layer of dust covers the whole tank.

A crewman of a PzKpfw III Ausf L command tank holds a wire rope towing cable as the tank moves up during the Kursk offensive of July 1943. Conversion of standard gun tanks to command vehicles gave headquarters crews a more effective defensive armament, since production command vehicles normally carried only machine guns for defense.

This overall Dark Yellow PzKpfw III Ausf L of 5.PzDiv carries the division sign in Yellow Ochre against a patch of Dark Gray on the hull tail plate next to the national insignia. This vehicle has been modified with a field-made stowage rack welded to the rear hull.

A group of PzKpfw III Ausf Ls move up a road in Russia during mid-1943. Most are fitted with full hull and turret skirts, and could be mistaken for PzKpfw IVs from a distance. All of these vehicles are Dark Yellow oversprayed with patches of Olive Green and Red Brown.

PANZER III AUSF M

The PzKpfw III Ausf M was the final production model of the basic PzKpfw III gun tank to enter production and was a modification of the Ausf L design. Originally 1000 PzKpfw III Ausf Ms were ordered, however, this order was reduced in anticipation of the introduction of the *Panzerkampfwagen* V Panther. The reduced effectiveness of the KwK39 L/60 gun in combat against the Soviet T-34 also led the Army to further reduce orders for the Ausf M. In the event, only 250 vehicles were completed as PzKpfw III Ausf M gun tanks, 165 hulls were set aside for use in StuG III production, 100 were built as PzKpfw III (Fl) flamethrower tanks, and still others were completed as PzKpfw III Ausf N support tanks armed with the 75MM L/24 howitzer.

The major difference between the Ausf L and Ausf M was the provision for deep wading. The Ausf M had the capability to wade water up to 4 ½ feet deep. The exhaust system was completely re-designed, with extended exhaust pipes similar to those on the *Tauchpanzer* III. The exhaust pipes ran into a cylindrical muffler equipped with a one-way float valve mounted high on the rear hull. The side mounted engine air intakes were fitted with cover plates and seals. To prepare for wading these covers were closed manually from outside the vehicle, however, they could be released by cables from inside the tank once it had reached dry ground. All hull intakes, exhausts, and vents had new seals installed and air for the engine was taken in through the fighting compartment using the turret ventilator system.

A number of detail changes were also introduced on the Ausf M. The headlights were repositioned from the glacis to a position on the fenders. Late production Ausf Ms were fitted with thin armor turret and hull skirts for protection against hollow-charge anti-tank rounds. The smoke candles under the tailplate were replaced by three 90MM smoke dischargers mounted on each side of the turret.

250 Ausf M gun tanks were delivered between late 1942 and early 1943 and were used primarily to replace combat losses during 1943. Chassis numbers were 76101-77800, although a number of reserved numbers were not used.

Panzer III Ausf M (Fl) Flammpanzer

During 1943 100 PzKpfw III Ausf Ms were built by MIAG and converted by Wegmann as PzKpfw III (Fl) flame thrower tanks. The main gun and internal ammunition stowage was replaced with a flame projector and fuel tanks. The effective range of the flame pro-

A column of PzKpfw III Ausf M tanks move up past infantry positions during the Don campaign in southern Russia. The first and third vehicles are Ausf Ms while the second tank is an Ausf J. The lead tank is fitted with turret smoke dischargers, spaced armor, and Bosch blackout headlights mounted on the fenders.

jector was 55-60 meters (164-196 feet) depending on weather conditions. Enough fuel was carried on board to allow approximately eighty one-two second bursts of flame.

The majority of PzKpfw III Ausf M (Fl)s had additional 30MM armor plates welded to the hull front, since they had to get close to their targets to use the flame projector. Chassis numbers ranged from 77609 through 77708 and the SdKfz number for the PzKpfw III Ausf M (Fl) was changed to SdKfz 141/3, again denoting a change in the vehicle's armament.

The PzKpfw III Ausf M (Fl) was assigned to special battalions, normally consisting of twenty to thirty tanks. Most saw action on the Eastern Front against fortified positions.

This PzKpfw III Ausf M command tank has been modified with a large sheet metal stowage rack on the engine decking. Command tanks could be identified by the extra radio antennas carried for communications with higher authority.

Rear Hull Wading Equipment

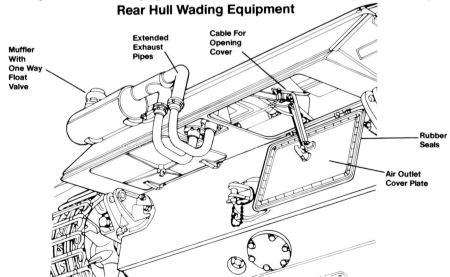

Muffler With One Way Float Valve

Extended Exhaust Pipes

Cable For Opening Cover

Rubber Seals

Air Outlet Cover Plate

A PzKpfw III Ausf M, believed to be of 24.PzDiv is halted along a dirt road during the southern Russian campaign of early 1943. The tank is overall Dark Yellow, covered with a thick layer of dust. The turret numbers and small Panzer rhomboid sign below the right side of the tailplate are in White.

A PzKpfw III Ausf M advances down a dirt road in Russia with the side air intake covers closed to keep out the clouds of dust thrown up by the tracks. The crew has hand painted an Olive Green pattern over the Dark Yellow base camouflage to help break up the vehicle's outline.

German troops made considerable use of identification training aids such as 1:20 scale paper identification models of Russian KV-1 tanks. These models, when finished, would allow the crew to practice vehicle identification from any angle.

Turret Smoke Dischargers

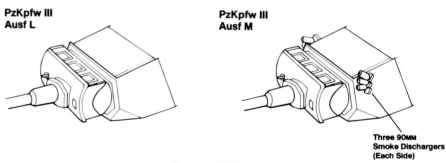

PzKpfw III
Ausf L

PzKpfw III
Ausf M

Three 90MM
Smoke Dischargers
(Each Side)

Armor Skirts

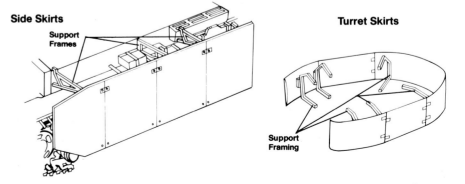

Side Skirts

Support Frames

Turret Skirts

Support Framing

This Dark Yellow and Olive Green PzKpfw III Ausf M of 2.PzDiv carries the division sign, a White trident, on the superstructure front near the crewman's boot. The shield on the turret side is the insignia of PzRgt 3. The eagle is Black with Yellow Ochre claws and beak. The small shield is Red with a White cross, and the larger shield is in White.

Headlights

PzKpfw III
Ausf L

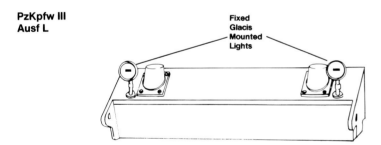

Fixed
Glacis
Mounted
Lights

PzKpfw III
Ausf M

Removable
Fender Mounted
Bosch Lights

A PzKpfw III Ausf M, followed by an Ausf J, advances through a Russian village during 1943. The Ausf M has an earlier style headlight in place of the starboard Bosch light. The camouflage is Dark Yellow oversprayed with patterns of Olive Green outlined in Red Brown and the turret numbers are in Red.

The *Flammenwerfer-Panzer* III Ausf M carried the same wading gear fitted to gun armed Ausf Ms. The high muffler is at the far left and the side air intakes are fitted with sealing flaps and their retainer frames. This tank is overall Dark Yellow, with Yellow Ochre numbers outlined in Black.

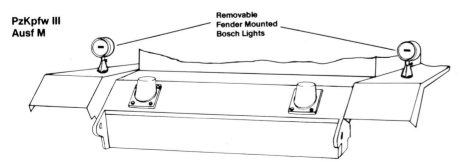

41

(Below) A *Flammenwerfer-Panzer* Ausf M tests its main armament before going into action. The flame projector was very effective against pill boxes and other fortifications, but the vehicle had to get in close in order to bring the weapon within effective range.

(Above) A PzKpfw III Ausf M (Fl) fires its main weapon, a flame projector with an effective range of 180-197 feet. The flame projector barrel was heavier than the 50mm L/60 gun barrel, but was hard to distinguish from the standard tank gun from a distance.

Flame Projector

PzKpfw III Ausf M

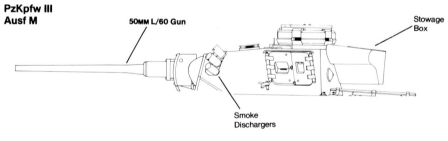

50mm L/60 Gun

Stowage Box

Smoke Dischargers

PzKpfw III Ausf M (Fl)

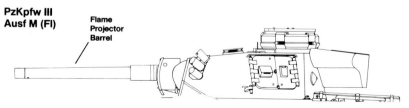

Flame Projector Barrel

PANZER III AUSF N SUPPORT TANK

The PzKpfw III Ausf N support tank was the final variant of the PzKpfw III and remained in production from late 1942 until August of 1943 when Panzer III production was terminated. These vehicles were built from existing PzKpfw III Ausf J, Ausf L, and Ausf M vehicles and were virtually identical to the corresponding gun tank except for the armament fitted. The original main gun was replaced by a short barreled 75MM L/24 howitzer and internal ammunition stowage revised to accommodate the different sized ammunition casings with a total of sixty-four rounds being carried.

The majority of Ausf Ns did not mount spaced armor on the gun mantlet because of the extra weight of the 75MM howitzer. Late production vehicles were fitted with a thicker cupola fitted with a one-piece hatch. During conversion fittings were added to allow thin armor skirting to be mounted on the turret and hull. Beginning in 1943 Ausf Ns began arriving from the factory covered with 220 pounds of 'Zimmerit' anti-magnetic mine paste.

The short barreled 75MM L/24 howitzer had been used in early models of the PzKpfw IV and was available in large numbers as PzKpfw IVs were up-gunned. The howitzer fired a more effective high explosive round than the 50MM KwK39 L/60 gun and, with the development of a special shaped-charge projectile, had better armor-piercing performance.

The success of the first Ausf Ns, built from PzKpfw III Ausf J (3) and Ausf L (447) tanks, led to the conversion of an addition 213 Ausf Ms plus another thirty-seven vehicles converted from various PzKpfw III variants that were returned to the factory for major overhaul or repair. A total of 700 Ausf Ns were produced between mid-1942 and August of 1943 with chassis numbers 73851-77800.

The Ausf N was used primarily in the fire support role in PzKpfw VI Tiger battalions and Panzer-Grenadier Divisions.

PzKpfw III Ausf N support tanks of sPzAbt 501 wait along side a road in Tunisia during late 1942. The Ausf N (based on the Ausf L chassis) has been fitted with a gun travel lock mounted on the superstructure decking. This vehicle is overall desert Brown, covered with a thick layer of dust with the turret numbers '113' in Red outlined in White.

This Ausf N support tank, built on a PzKpfw III Ausf L chassis, is unusual in that it has spaced armor on the gun mantlet. The wire mount on the cupola is an anti-aircraft mount for a MG 34 machine gun. The tank is camouflaged overall Dark Yellow, with White turret numbers.

Turret

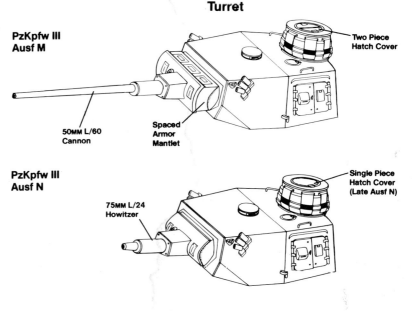

PzKpfw III Ausf M

50MM L/60 Cannon

Spaced Armor Mantlet

Two Piece Hatch Cover

PzKpfw III Ausf N

75MM L/24 Howitzer

Single Piece Hatch Cover (Late Ausf N)

A PzKpfw III Ausf N support tank of sPzAbt 501 waits alongside a Tunisian road for the word that the way is clear of mines. The jerry cans carried on the field installed stowage rack on the rear deck are for water not fuel.

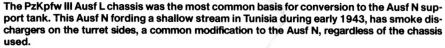

The PzKpfw III Ausf L chassis was the most common basis for conversion to the Ausf N support tank. This Ausf N fording a shallow stream in Tunisia during early 1943, has smoke dischargers on the turret sides, a common modification to the Ausf N, regardless of the chassis used.

PzKpfw III Ausf N support tanks were used to protect Tiger tanks from enemy infantry and anti-tank units. The sand bags on the front plate are carried for protection against shaped-charge weapons, such as the American bazooka rocket launcher. The turret numbers '07' are in Red outlined in White.

This PzKpfw III Ausf N (converted Ausf M) hulk continues to serve —as a target vehicle for training tank gunners. There are at least six shell holes in the front of the vehicle.

PANZERBEFEHLSWAGEN III

From the earliest days of the German armored forces the Army realized that specialized command vehicles would be required to direct the movement of large armor formations. The *Kleiner Panzerbefehlswagen* (small armored command vehicle), based on the PzKpfw I Ausf B chassis, was found to be too small to accommodate the variety of radio equipment necessary to manage a large scale tank assault. To provide high ranking armor officers with a vehicle capable of accompanying the armor force and large enough to carry the necessary communications equipment, a command version of the PzKpfw III chassis was developed under the designation *Grosser Panzerbefehlswagen* III.

In an effort to avoid drawing unwanted attention to the command tank, the PzBefWg III was constructed to externally resemble a standard PzKpfw III gun tank. The turret was fixed and bolted to the hull with a dummy gun mantlet and main gun (simulating a 37MM L/46.5 tank gun). Extra vision and pistol ports were installed in the superstructure sides and a pistol port replaced the hull machine gun mount. Armor protection was increased to 30MM all around — twice the thickness of an early PzKpfw III. The turret interior was fitted with radios and a folding map table.

Radio equipment installed included the Fu 13, Fu 6, and Fu 7 ultra shortwave radio and Fu 8 medium wave transceiver. Some variants were equipped with ground to air radios for coordination with *Luftwaffe* air support aircraft. The usual crew complement was five; commander, staff officer, two radio operators, and the driver.

Other specialized equipment included two whip antennas, one 29.5 foot retractable radio mast, and a large frame antenna on the engine deck behind the fixed turret. Defensive armament consisted of a flexible MG 34 machine gun in a ball mount on the false gun mantlet.

The first thirty PzBefWg IIIs were based on the PzKpfw III Ausf D chassis and were designated *Panzerbefehlswagen* III Ausf D1 (SdKfz 267/268) with chassis numbers 60341-60370. These were first used in Poland and France, however, their poor suspension led to early retirement after the French campaign.

The second group of PzBefWg IIIs built consisted of forty-five vehicles based on the PzKpfw III Ausf E chassis under the designation *Panzerbefehlswagen* III Ausf E (SdKfz 266-268, chassis numbers 60501-60545). The lower hull was identical to the PzKpfw III tank with the superstructure and fixed turret being very similar to the PzBefWg III Ausf D1. The PzBefWg III Ausf E was very successful and was first used in the invasions of the Low Countries and France during 1940. Surviving vehicles continued to be used until the end of the war, although most were eliminated by attrition.

The third order for PzBefWg IIIs was based on the PzKpfw III Ausf H chassis. 145 vehicles were built between late 1940 and the fall of 1941, with a further thirty vehicles produced during the winter of 1941-42. Chassis numbers were 70001-70145 and 70146-70175.

The PzBefWg III Ausf H was very similar in appearance to the Ausf E with the major difference being the addition of 30MM applique armor bolted to the hull front and rear, and on the superstructure front plate. 400MM tracks were fitted to many vehicles during production and still others were retrofitted with wide tracks during overhauls. Early vehicles carried a false mantlet and dummy gun tube that simulated the 37MM L/46.5 gun while later versions had a dummy gun installation resembling the 50MM KwK L/42 gun. An observation periscope was mounted in the turret roof so the commander could observe the battlefield while remaining under armor.

The PzBefWg III Ausf H entered service in 1941 and although losses were heavy on the Eastern front, nearly two thirds of the PzBefWg III Ausf H built remained in service nearly a year after OPERATION BARBAROSSA was launched.

In 1942, eighty-one PzKpfw III Ausf J tanks were ordered converted to command tanks by reducing internal ammunition stowage to make room for the required radio equipment. These conversions gave command tank crews a standard tank gun for self-defense. From 1943 on, all replacement command vehicles were produced by converting existing PzKpfw III gun tanks to the command tank configuration. 104 additional command tanks, mounting the KwK L/42 gun, were converted in 1943 with chassis numbers ranging from 72001 to 74100. Eventually, tanks mounting the KwK39 L/60 were also converted to command vehicle configuration by removing an ammunition rack and installing a long-range radio set in its place. The prominent frame antenna, which was found to betray the vehicle's true role, was replaced by a rod antenna with a star array at the top. This antenna was ha ' 'r to see from a distance and was less likely to attract enemy attention to the vehicle.

Armored Observation Vehicles

The development of self-propelled artillery vehicles led to a requirement for a mobile protected observation vehicle for use in directing artillery fire. To meet this requirement, a number of obsolete PzKpfw IIIs were converted for use as *Panzerbeobachtungswagen* (armored observation vehicles).

These vehicles were modified with additional 30MM armor plate on the hull front and rear of all early models converted (Ausf E through G). The hull MG 34 machine gun was removed and the mount filled in. The original turret mantlet and gun were removed and a thicker mantlet was installed. This mantlet carried a dummy gun tube installed in the position of the former co-axial MG 34 machine gun and a flexible MG 34 was mounted in the center of the mantlet in the position formerly occupied by the main gun.

A total of 262 PzBeobWg IIIs were converted from a variety of PzKpfw III variants between early 1943 and the Spring of 1944. Chassis numbers were drawn from the normal range of PzKpfw III numbers (Ausf E to Ausf M). These vehicles were assigned to Hummel and Wespe SP artillery battalions beginning in early 1943 and served until the end of the war.

German staff officers confer alongside a PzBefWg III Ausf D1 command vehicle of 4.PzDiv during the Polish campaign. The conical pistol port in the hull machine gun position, flexible MG 34 in the dummy turret mantlet, and large frame antenna are identification features of the PzBefWg III.

A PzBefWg III Ausf D1 of 2.PzDiv advances past a German checkpoint on a French road during 1940. The division sign, two Yellow Ochre dots, is just below the White rhomboid on the glacis. The 'Div' marking next to the rhomboid in White indicates this tank belongs to the division Headquarters unit.

A PzBefWg III Ausf D1 passes an eighteen ton tractor on a road in Poland. The complex leaf suspension system of the Ausf D1 was less than satisfactory and these vehicles were quickly withdrawn from service during 1941.

Panzer Befehlswagen III Development

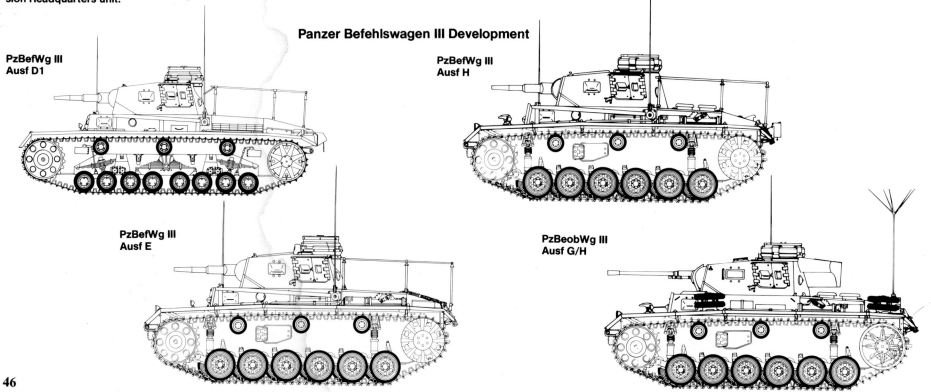

PzBefWg III
Ausf D1

PzBefWg III
Ausf H

PzBefWg III
Ausf E

PzBeobWg III
Ausf G/H

This PzBefWg III Ausf E of 1.PzDiv slid into a water filled shell hole and became bogged down. Every effort was made to make the PzBefWg III look like a standard gun tank, however, the large frame radio antenna betrayed their real role as command vehicles. (NARS)

A PzBefWg III Ausf E of 9.PzDiv advances along a muddy road in Russia during the opening phases of OPERATION BARBAROSSA, the invasion of Russia. The division tactical sign on the superstructure plate is in Yellow Ochre.

Staff officers hold a conference on the turret roof of a PzBefWg III Ausf E in Russia during early 1941. The jerry cans on the turret roof are for extra water and the extra track sections are secured in place on the hull front with welded bars.

PzBefWg III Rack Antenna

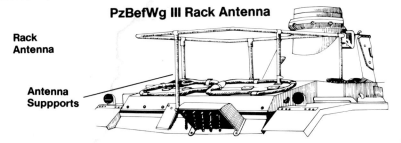

Rack Antenna

Antenna Suppports

47

An overall Dark Gray PzBefWg III Ausf H of 2.PzDiv advances down a Greek road at high speed. This vehicle carries bolted-on armor plate on the glacis and hull front plate along with spare track links on the superstructure front, top, and hull front plate.

A PzBefWg III Ausf H passes through a Balkan village during 1941. The vehicle is Dark Gray with a heavy layer of dust. The White name *Kastor* has been painted on the turret side in Old Gothic lettering. 'fu 6u.8' in White on the superstructure front plate identified the type of radio equipment carried.

The crew of this PzBefWg III Ausf H of 9.PzDiv takes advantage of a quiet moment on the Russian Front to get some sleep. The semi-circle mounts on the engine deck rear are spare road wheel stowage brackets. The vehicle is overall Dark Gray with a Yellow Ochre division sign on the port side of the rear plate.

A snow camouflaged PzBefWg III passes through a Russian forest during the Winter of 1943-44. The identification markings have been left on the turret skirting in Yellow Ochre against patches of the base color, Dark Yellow.

PzBeobWg III Mantlet

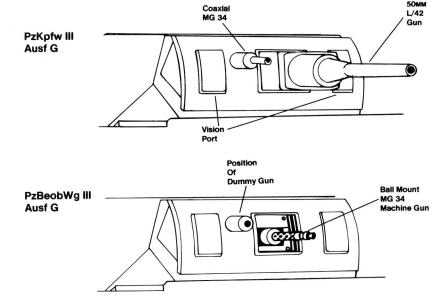

PzKpfw III Ausf G

Coaxial MG 34

50MM L/42 Gun

Vision Port

PzBeobWg III Ausf G

Position Of Dummy Gun

Ball Mount MG 34 Machine Gun

A *Panzerbeobachtungswagen* III (armored observation vehicle) moves down a dirt road in Russia during 1943. PzBeobWg III Ausf Gs carried extra armor plate on the front and rear of the vehicle, a dummy gun in place of the co-axial MG 34 machine gun and a flexible MG 34 centrally mounted in the mantlet.

WWII Armor "in action"

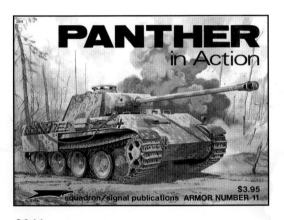

2011

2012

2027

2016

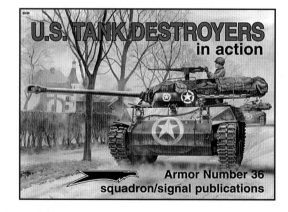

2036

squadron/signal publications